Seán Haldane was born in 194.
Ireland. He was educated at th
Institution and University Colleg
ated with First Class Honours in I
Canada, where he was co-founde
Quebec, which published poetry a... criticism. At that time he
was also a part-time farmer and university lecturer in English.
Subsequently he studied psychology, in which he obtained his
Ph.D. from the Saybrook Institute in San Francisco. He has
worked as a private psychotherapist and then as a clinical
psychologist (with a particular interest in neuropsychology)
in Prince Edward Island and in British Columbia, where he
lives at present.

Among Seán Haldane's published works are:

The Coast and Inland (1968)
Homage to Trumbull Stickney (1968)
The Fright of Time (1970)
The Ocean Everywhere (1970)
What Poetry Is (1970)
Skindiving (1972)
Emotional First Aid (1984)

Desire in Belfast

Seán Haldane

THE
BLACKSTAFF
PRESS

ACKNOWLEDGEMENTS

Some of these poems have appeared in the *Scotsman*, the *Spectator*, and in an earlier collection, *The Coast and Inland* (1968).

First published in 1992 by
The Blackstaff Press Limited
3 Galway Park, Dundonald, Belfast BT16 0AN, Northern Ireland
with the assistance of
The Arts Council of Northern Ireland

© Seán Haldane, 1992
All rights reserved

Typeset by Textflow Services Limited

Printed by The Guernsey Press Company Limited

British Library Cataloguing in Publication Data
Haldane, Seán
Desire in Belfast
I. Title
821. 914

ISBN   0-85640-496-9

CONTENTS

1
DESIRE IN BELFAST

Invocation	3
Desire in Belfast	4
Thunder	9
Rhododendrons	10
Quatrains	12
Peeping Tom	13
Naming truth	14
The bullhead	15
Cave Hill	17
Yes, rage	18
My way	19
Fragments	20
At Brú na Bóinne (Newgrange)	22
At Struell Wells	23
Mourne	24
The cry	25
The blackbird	26

2
A COUNTRY WITHOUT NAME

A country without name	31
What women do	33
'A matter of time'	35
Acrobats	36
Shells	37
&	38

Zero	39
The storeroom	40
In gratitude for the General	41
Mind, mind	45
This moment	46
Pastoral	47
Dán	48
Honesty	49
Solomon	50
Entranced	51

3

THE DOUBLE-GOER

The double-goer	55
Vortices	57
Islands	58
Devourer	59
Ambition	60
Poor Ball	61
Jack and Jenny	62
Grammar of love	63
An immigrant	64
Mantis	65
Cascades	66
Hedge and wall	68
Avebury	69

4

LETTER FROM NEW IRELAND

Baie des chaleurs	73
Letter from New Ireland	75
You and island	77
Man	78

Waves	79
Cousins Shore	80
Micmac woman	82
Dieland	83
Terra firma	84
Thank-you note	85
Debt	86
Sunstruck	87
Icy road	88
The murmur	90
Accents	91
Quince	93

1
DESIRE IN BELFAST

INVOCATION

O swimming vegetables by the Smithfield market
And urine running down the legs of women
At the bus stops, O lowering hills of Belfast –
Never stop raining: sun would see too much.

O rolling in the bunkers of rained-out golf courses
In the gritty sand of our so fierce repentance,
We thank thee for thy weather, O Belfast –
Never stop raining: sun would see us bare.

And O our smell would come surging out of us
With no baffle of musty rain-soaked wool
To keep it in, and O we'd be ashamed –
Never stop raining: sun would see us flesh.

And O the roses would no longer grow
In McGredy's gardens, petals would fall to dust,
The thorny briars of our hearts' veins exposed –
Never stop raining: sun would see us die.

DESIRE IN BELFAST

Hothouse of desire,
In the Botanic Gardens,
Jungle damp, steaming pipes, banana fronds,
Against the railing of the goldfish pond,
Leaning back, she pulled up her dress,
Round-bellied as a Hindu goddess.

Volumes of desire,
Behind the shelves of the Linen Hall Library,
She sitting on my knee reading Dante,
'He kissed my mouth all trembling'
(*La bocca mi baciò tutto tremante*).

School of desire,
Waiting for me in the park, her uniform skirt
Unbuttoned, underthings in her satchel –
We'd lie on leaves in the dirt.

Bush of desire,
Rhododendron dripping on us bare,
Blood-coloured petals caught in her hair.

Flowers of desire,
Hydrangeas in the suburbs,
'Like blue notepaper,' she said –
Us writing our story in fallen hawthorn petals,
Printing it in the crushed daisies and buttercups
We made our bed.

Reservoir of desire,
Children and pensioners playing with model boats,
Us on a wrought-iron bench,
Hands in each other's clothes under our coats.

Tears of desire,
Opening her blouse for me to hold
Her breasts, backed in a thorn hedge,
Crying in the cold.

Concert of desire,
At recitals or the symphony,
Thinking of afterwards – against a wall
In the dark puddles of an entry.

Journey of desire,
The last Cave Hill bus at night,
On the back seat of the empty upper deck,
My eye on the round mirror above the stairs,
Her fingernails dug into my neck.

Dance of desire,
Quickstepping in the Floral Hall,
Two animals on hind legs in a clinch,
Or waltzing at the Lifeboat Ball
In evening dress, Lily of the Valley scent –
Later we'd stroke each other inch by inch.

Song of desire,
The blackbird at Island Mahee

Which brought a saint eternity,
Us among the brambles kissing,
Purple-mouthed with blackberry.

River of desire,
The Lagan, factories wrecked by Luddite time,
Gladed by nettles, burrs, thorns,
Millwheels stopped in slime,
A muddy dell, us crouching in the mire.

Hill of desire,
Woods, sheeps' paths, caves, paper and shit,
Peeping Toms . . . On the summit
Us hidden, heather and gorse on fire.

Lane of desire,
Buttermilk Loney, where before the Twelfth
Townies dragged down branches for the bonfires
(And groped the two retarded sisters
From the white, half-doored cottage),
She stepping around the cowpats
And singing 'À la claire fontaine' –
Her mouth I had mouthed.

Rain of desire,
Pouring down the windows of the car
We locked ourselves in
Parked off the Hightown Road on the moors
(B Specials patrolled in Land-Rovers with Sten guns),
Lying skin to skin.

City of desire,
Us walking hand in hand
('Stand still ye sinners!'
Bellowed at us by a soapbox preacher),
Half a million rages
Rising with the smoke from chimneys,
The air sparkling between our eyes.

Poems of desire,
Graves (one story and one story only),
Blake's *Book of Thel*, Rilke's autumn day, Goethe
Tapping hexameters on his mistress's shoulder,
Breton's woman with the woodfire in her hair,
Me to her (from her? through her?), how spring would pass,
May blossom shivering from the tree
Falling white on grass.

Stones of desire,
The dolmen in the Giant's Ring
Among the chocolate wrappers
And broken bottles glistening
By moonlight, us in our blanket, trembling.

Stars of desire,
Orion ungirding his sword,
The rising Milky Way –
Sheathed in her I lay.

Coals of desire,
In January, heating a borrowed room,

Bursting frozen pipes in the attic,
Ceiling plaster falling onto the bed,
Icy water pouring on us naked.

Death of desire,
My disgust
– Not at lust –
At her sticky, tender love.
Recalled after thirty years
It brings me to tears.

THUNDER

Oh Mummy hold my hand in the thunder.
Alone, through the windowpane
He saw the ball of fire
Float down through grey rain.
It popped above the ground.

Later he searched and found
Only a small scorched mark
Like another made years before
By a dud German incendiary.

And when the iron balls of thunder
Trundled and rumbled round the horizon
He no longer needed Mummy.

O ball of fire, glow in my chest and belly
As I walk in this black city.

RHODODENDRONS

I buried a frog under a rhododendron.
I'd thrown it against the pebble-dashed wall
Of the house my parents were quarrelling in.
At times I disinterred it, stinking,
To study what death did, the corpse shrinking
And cut through by the skeleton.

My cat Boots, for fear he'd smother
My baby brother, had been put to sleep.
My dog Pip too – he'd got distemper
And St Vitus's dance. My godfather
Left me a hedgehog in the rubbish bin.
It had fleas, I kept it in a wire-mesh run
And tried to love it as it tried to dig
Its way out and succeeded one night,
Leaving me to the porcelain guardian angel
Beside my bed and my green night-light.

Now I'm with you under a rhododendron,
Our legs like frogs', the flowers weep,
And into the earth a kind of death
Seems to throw us with each outbreath.

I come back. You've killed me. I hate you
Until I see your eyes, puzzled as mine
When I murdered the frog, cared for the hedgehog,
And slept fitfully with my guardian angel –
Until the night a wall plug exploded

With a bang and a flash of sparkling blue
And I ran screaming down the stairs
To my mother's warm hands on my head.

Was it this I was fighting against,
And if I've found it now, my love,
Will my father's thumping footsteps come again
And I be wrenched pleading from you and led
Down rainslicked roads into the city of men?

And you be left, your face a streak in the dark,
Your tears part of the all-blurring rain . . . ?

I want to forget the whole story,
Get it out of my jolted brain
And come to you as now, but I'm afraid.
How easy it is for us to let go
Of this soaked world around
Us and dissolve into the ground.

QUATRAINS

We stood by the dolmen tomb,
Death fell to the grass:
A sprig of hawthorn bloom.
Our love would pass.

Under a hawthorn in May
We pushed our fate away,
Clutched each other fast
And trembling lay.

Lying in crimson heather
We defy all weather:
Mountains wet, or dry in sun,
Horses in pounding circles run.

PEEPING TOM

I felt his look. 'Get off with you,' I snarled.
He laughed but took a step back nervously
Licking his lips, then said, 'How old are youse?
Sixteen? You should be ashamed of yourselves.'

I was ashamed. My girl grabbed her raincoat
And pulled it over us. We lay there small
Under him. 'Should be ashamed,' he said.
Then, one hand in his trouser pocket,
He stumbled off into the miles of sky,
And left us on those moors ruffled by wind,
The heather flowers pink around my head.

NAMING TRUTH

Everything a lie except this lie,
This act we told ourselves was naked truth
And only truth: there never would be other.
And yet there was another and another
You and I: layers of slippery skin
Sloughed off revealed new layers underneath.
As snakes we proved endless, no tail or head,
And loved to wear us out, to kill, to die –
Tired by truth. And love turned into *love*
And as *love* withered: so the final truth
Was two and two and two and always two –
Seán and R———.

THE BULLHEAD

Fishing where the cold, vicious tide
Swept between rocky islands, I dragged in
A bullhead, spiny, with lurid scales.
I cut it off the hook and threw it back.

That month on the same coast, changed in sun,
She and I found beaches of pure coral
And swam in that sea whose foam
Stung our bodies, quickening desire.
At evening we stepped through walls,
Lifting the stones aside with shaky hands,
To find a patch of grass and blown bog cotton
Where we could lie in shadow cast by boulders
As the sun went down and spilled its fire.

One night we ate dulse, then drank poteen. Rage
At her once faithlessness burned in my brain.
I turned and staggered, shoved her to the ground.
Then we walked back together in cold shame.

Next day we crossed by boat to Inishmore,
She gaily singing to the other men,
And when we climbed to Dun Aengus fort
I muttered to myself I'd smash her head
On the sharp teeth of the chevaux-de-frise:
Each spike of stone went straight into my heart.

Desperately I tugged her behind the wall
Of the fort and pulled her to the grass,

Begging to have her hold me. She refused.
Then we all lay together on the cliff
Three hundred feet above the emerald sea.
I felt myself vertiginously dragged
Close to the edge, while she talked happily
And flirted with my friends, taking one's hand
And reading in the lines. I'd nothing to say,
I didn't belong up on the sunny land:
No more that spiny fish, my jealousy.

She wept in silence when I turned away.

CAVE HILL

Off Napoleon's Nose I fall,
Past the mouths of caves,
The sheeps' paths,
Hummocks of gorse, brambles,
A fake baronial castle,
A chapel, churches, -
Brick houses, ribbon roads,
The railway by the shore . . .
Splat.
In pools the lugworms wave
Their heads like tufted flowers,
Gulls drift like bog cotton,
Crabs squat like funerary urns,
Soon the polluted tide
Will choke me, stir my hair
With lugworms in the murk,
A nest for sidling crabs,
The gulls lost above
As I sink through the mud
Away from where she
Screams from the cliff edge
'Why did you leave me?'

YES, RAGE

Rage to get the moment back,
Smash your knuckles till they crack
Against the wall of stone, smack
Your head upon the chevaux-de-frise,
Grovel on your muddy knees,
Dribble grief onto the sod,
Stuff your pizzle in a clod,
Shriek to seagulls or to God,
Crack your nails down to the quick
Tearing at your shrunken prick,
Rage to get the moment back,
In mind's eye spiral through the black
To where she lies and dies in wrack,
Lashed, splashed and battered on the strand,
Cast over cliff top by your hand,
She clawed the puffins from their nests
And scraped the white skin off her breasts,
Slithered down the gullies, down
To crash in pounding wave crests, drown . . .
You lack the guts to throw yourself
After her from this towering shelf,
So howl and lacerate your pelt
And clutch and thump and wail your woe
While she dies where you dare not go –
Yes, rage to get the moment back.

MY WAY

I let the world flow through me while I go on my own way,
Not hardening to isolate myself, time-sculptured rock,
Nor scattered in the fields of space like shards of potters' clay,
I pick my way past bones, I skirt the haunted souterrain,
I squelch past yellow flags, I climb the crumbling limestone
    cliffs,
I stride across the moors, feet crunching heather scorched by
    fires,
I let the silver loughs, the sea, and mountains through my
    eyes,
The wind beating in my ears and tugging at my hair,
I search for her and call for her across the swirling skies.

FRAGMENTS

1

We lay together among the rain-soaked larches
In the dark of cloud-topped mountains.
Remember now the rush of dammed-up floods
When you cried out you loved me.

2

As if a wave had cast you ashore,
You lay on the beach of the bed,
Crannies tufted with crinkly dulse:
Even land-bound you contained the sea.

3

You taught me to take you slowly,
Not violently as before,
To let the feeling swim in us,
Not driving stormily
But curling over and over
On a hidden shore
Until it dissolved in waves . . .
But then our mouths tore
Breath from each other
And our hearts let go,
The beating everywhere,
Us lost in the flow.

4

'My heart came down to meet you there,' you say.
We lie sheet-shrouded, struck by moonlight
Through the glass cold as your eyes.
Your heart moves again as outside the door
In the dark stairwell my rival
Whimpers and cries.

5

We sat and talked in a public park
And watched your children playing in the sun,
But my thoughts were of the ancient world of dark
Where birds woke and twittered as we passed
Along the Lagan towpath, and at your will
A fish leapt suddenly, splashing silver
In the moon's deathlight. We touched and kissed,
The knife beside me used by you to kill.

AT BRÚ NA BÓINNE (NEWGRANGE)

I, the sun, shone over the spiralled threshold,
Probed my way along the narrow floor
Into the inmost corbelled vault
And spilled my warm drops in a granite bowl:
I am that man, daubed in red,
And she, with flint knife, pale, eyes like stone,
The always chilly, mirroring, menstrual moon.

AT STRUELL WELLS

Toadflax and maidenhair
From the cracks in the wall
And the stone stair:
My heart wells as I recall
You there.

MOURNE

The mountains black, heather had lost its bloom
Above the silent lake where we came
Below the threatening scree, and in that gloom
Your red skirt flickered like a flame.

I forgot. But when I returned alone
My stomach stabbed in sudden memory,
My heart froze in that immensity of stone,
And time was nothing, nothing then to me.

I'd had my reasons to destroy us, known
Even, as now, that they were good,
But longed for you in sickness as I stood.

THE CRY

Three counties – Antrim, Down, Tyrone,
Three loughs – Belfast, Strangford, Neagh,
Two mountain ranges – Sperrins, Mournes,
And two countries – green Ireland
And blue Scotland on the sea . . .

And under streaks of smog, the city:
We could hear its whisper
Even through the roar of wind,
The strange internal sizzle from our eyes
When we looked at each other,
Our longing going out as if a cry
Across the world – mountains, loughs and sea,
Beyond Scotland – even to this country.

THE BLACKBIRD

The entry where we courting stood
Is stained with lovers' blood,
Across the Bog Meadows, bombs
And bullets break flesh for tombs,
The red buses we used to burn
Inside are charred with real fire,
The pub's become a funeral pyre.
O love, our childish moans
Are nothing to the groans
Of death.
      Don't you return
Unless as ashes in an urn
For scattering in that country,
The grimy walls of that entry
Are blown to dust, cobblestones
Dashed with bits of rag and bones,
Along the alleys where we'd stroll
'Pigs' grind, of soldiers on patrol,
Walking's under machine guns' eyes,
It's not my hands between your thighs
Would melt you, body-searchers would pet
You at the barbed-wire barrier's net,
The shop you'd buy clothes I'd discover
With trembling hands is boarded over,
The coffee house where we'd gaze
Knee to knee and plan our days
Is blasted to smithereens,
The waitresses, linen aprons,

All to bits, in rubble, so lives
Trickle where they can't be cleaned
In the gutters of the mind,
The one more slowly dying place
A smile, the beauty of a face,
A welcoming, survives.
                        Don't you return
If there's one granule left to burn,
But mind us on the hills
Where clasped as one we'd view
(Narrow your eyes as you used to)
This land, the great city below,
Pink terrace houses row on row,
The chimney stacks of mills,
The cracks of streets and entries –
Pottinger's, Joy's – the gantries
Looming on Queen's Island, bridges
To County Down's green ridges,
The Lagan's silver arm, the lough,
See as we saw them in our day
The whins, the hawthorns where we lay,
Hear as we heard –
    A small bird
    Whistling piped
    From sharp beak
    Pure yellow,
    Casts a cry
    On Loch Laig,
    Black from twig
    By meadow –

And let the winds from the Atlantic
Tamed by the Sperrins to pulsing air
Ruffle your sun-flecked hair,
And think of me: I'll not be long,
I listen to the same blackbird's song.

The indented lines are a translation of the medieval Irish poem 'Int én bec', known as 'The Blackbird of Belfast Lough'.

2
A COUNTRY WITHOUT NAME

A COUNTRY WITHOUT NAME

In a country without name the princess lies
Beneath the stones and grass with gentian starred,
On slopes below the pending avalanche,
The gentian tubers rooted in her eyes.

She dreams of violated rooms, doors shattered,
The crenellations vitreously melted
By thunderbolts, the faces bled and blanched
Of men-at-arms in pieces struck and scattered.

And now insects invade the sanctuary
Her thighs once guarded chaste as statuary,
They pry within her chamber and unmake
The pillars of her lost virginity.

And now the snow-shrouds trickle into flood,
And men-at-arms begin to twitch awake,
Their blackened fingers locked on rusty swords,
The brown soil crumbling in a stream of blood.

The princess moves, she breathes, her nipples rise
Like new pink buds, the earth and grass divide.
Slowly she stands upright, then horrified
Invokes the flowers of springtime to appease

The raised and trickling swords above her head:
She promises the gentians of her eyes,

The snowdrops of her skin, the buds, and last
The dusky hellebore between her thighs.

Enfolded, one by one, each warrior dies.
The flowers burst, the avalanches boom,
And she returns enshrouded to her tomb.

WHAT WOMEN DO

Così fan tutte: so all women do.
But when I was thirteen I wasn't sure
What they did. In the opera they fell
For army officers. Divine duets
Vibrated in the Salzburg night air.

In front of me was a little Austrian girl
With serious eyes and straight brown hair.
We never spoke. I thought of her as Suzanne
When I remembered her (and I did),
Still not sure what women do.

In Vienna I saw *Tannhäuser*
In the overheated, overgilded Staatsoper.
A woman sitting next to me was blue,
Literally, and smelt of some sickening scent,
To cover dying, I supposed.
A soprano shrieked from a papier-mâché hill:
The Venusberg. Her fat, veiled body quivered.
Was this what women do?

Wagner wrote music – swelled with fame,
Inhaling his mistress's scented handkerchief
As he set out words and notes: the Master.
Music wrote Mozart – to death,
Moving through him in coaches and in taverns,
Forcing his cramped fingers to write it down.

Rolling with fever on summer nights in town
While his sweet Costanza played tricks at the spa
With her army officer, Mozart knew
What women do.

Sweet Suzanne of the serious eyes,
Do you remember me when you hear
Così fan tutte? So all women do –
And all men too:
We disappear.

'A MATTER OF TIME'

She loved me. I loved her. It ended. Now
One eye hides behind a leaf, the other
Stares from photocopy-pigment soot.
Is she alive? The repro doesn't tell.
There's no fragrance in a xerox smell.

A xerox of a xerox of a xerox . . .
Irradiated love . . . By what nerve gas,
What blastless neutron warfare was it killed?
So wails the lover lost and losing: I.
Toxins and X-rays de-marrowed my bones
And weakened muscles like a fluorescent.
Inside myself I pulled her down to hell,
Not outside on those crushed glades of bluebell,
Not in that cold dawn when she came to bed
And gave me one last time the flower I'd bled.

Gone (click), gone (click), gone (click), gone (click),
   gone (click) . . .
Layers of xerox back in time's machine,
'It ended.' No. Gone (click). I ended it.
As love it started. I made it obscene.
And now I try to make a xerox clean.

ACROBATS

Snow whirls around my ankles in a gust
Of wind sweeping across the icy crust.
I cannot cry your name, it is too far.
Let the message from my frozen feet go through
My boots then crusts of ice and earth and spar
Thousands of molten miles then out to you
And up through your bare feet before I fall:
We are unwilling acrobats on this ball.

SHELLS

Mussels, faded blue, and crab shells, red,
And whelks, broken – the bland waves
In lazily regular white lines
Throw up their dead.

Inland to a sky of cloudy glass
People raise parched throats,
And insects, in shells living,
Seethe in the grass.

Our lobsters hiss as they turn red,
Boiling like martyred cardinals,
As I uncork the wine
And butter bread.

We seem unmoved by the lobsters' hells,
Our own skin burning red from sun,
But our hearts shrink inside
Their cheerful shells.

Soon we must leave for inland
Where skin will peel in shards
To withered grass, and our fixed smiles
Recall this ocean, bland.

&

Time is unfeeling, not hot, not cold,
Not alive, not dead, but everywhere
Fusing cells, jostling them apart,
Driving us together, shoving us aside,
Indifferent to the weeping from the heart.

Its measured science is without a con:
Never itself withstanding, just its clear
Knowing, pushing blindly – no recall
And no persuading it ever to stop
Its constant restless pro and probing all.

And all we set against it is our skin,
Stretched and battered like a tympanum
By its relentless wave-pulse, so intense
We clutch each other fast as we let go,
All trace in us dissolved of present tense.

Flotsam and jetsam of our bodies drift
Behind us on the sea of memory,
As waking lustrous eyes and tender hands
Form bridges for the new words *you* and *I*,
Our fingers interlaced like ampersands.

ZERO

A zero is a no to time,
A no an O with bounds with rounds.
The time-seed cannot pierce its cell
To swell a ball, since cell is wall
Or nothing, swept by wave or all
Its O shrunk from surrounding what –
Pull/pushed to what is/what is not.

A zero is an O a yes
Which opens lips to time's ingress,
Becomes its form, its outer skin
(Pulsating genesis within)
And not a gap, no micro-chasm
With blade-thin space, but tissue slides
And rolls together rippled sides.

The membrane of so-called zero
Holds tubules, vesicles in plasm
Moiled on each other oiled by flow,
Cyclosis of the jism, and spasm:
The outside pushed, the inside pulled,
Both coupled in the yes of time –
The inescapable colloidal slime.

THE STOREROOM

Time rushes on, I choke in dust,
My hands clutch at the shelf
Of my unpublished manuscript
In this room without windows,
Cold-floored as a crypt.

Letters from old friends flutter down
With curious out-of-date stamps.
I wonder where time took them.
(This one, an ex-poet, drunkenly fell
And smashed in a stairwell.)

My fingers touch the ribboned bundles
Of love letters: do they breathe now,
Those breasts I died upon? That brown
Hair must be greying I used to smell
Fresh as a gosling's down.

The writing comes from gentle hands
That have touched me: do they mould now?
Worms thread the sinews of the palms
And pass dust through in graveyard holes
Where throats are burrowed in by moles.

IN GRATITUDE FOR THE GENERAL

The Elect who followed in the General's track,
His last mad rush to gain more territory,
Ran more risks than the bullets at their back:
Not all the villages were pacified.
Angry officials claim them but at night
Shiver inside, playing chess to smother
The clamorous beat of hearts longing for mother.

As leaves vibrate in the bush, birds call,
Or enemy throats, natives' blowpipes avenge
The exemplary corpses newly hung
In the village square to proclaim control:
The villagers remember the General.

He fraternised with some, slept with their women,
Though openly at midday through the square
Would promenade his straight-backed, perfect wife,
Defying every hostile, knowing stare.
Some of the children playing in the mud
Show his characteristic marble eyes
And dominating nose. One broken woman
Still limps from when in drunken despair
He threw her down a high veranda stair.

Officials parrot his ideology;
It is said the Capo's directorial suit,
His deputies' shirts, jackets and ties
Come from the General's trunkful of supplies.

In the city – where he had gone laden with maps
And strange devices, marbled rocks, odd plants,
To promote his finds – accused of playing God,
The General was shot by a firing squad.

The war between the villages and city
Is so old no one knows when it began,
Although the General himself would say
It started with his first rebellion.
Always moving along, he could not stay
In either village or city, each campaign
Would draw him further into new terrain.

The Elect followed his path. The dangers:
Mantraps, crazed loss, disorientation,
Visions, mirages of floating mountains,
Lakes which dimmed to swamps, wrens like condors
Looming with cyclonic shifts of light,
And then the terror of the sudden night.

On the journey no rewards except the greetings
And kind handclasps of passing savages
Who recognised them: in the lakes' mirrors
They looked the same, bronzed and dishevelled,
Lithe as animals, cunning in their eyes.
Until they reached the high frontier, the stars –
As if they entered a new universe.

This, then, is where the General came
On that final survey trip from which he returned

Raving with his caravan of goods.
The Elect can learn from him: not to go back.
Sanity hangs on not trusting old friends,
Not trying to convince: bulldozers rust,
Skeletons in their seats, on the foothill track,
Recalling the final greedy thrust
Of city into new territory,
Using the General's hastily drawn maps,
His converted guerrilla villagers
Fleeing from the cruel pillagers.

Fanatic village officials with their bust
Of the General, and their in-house gossip
About the length of his penis, his sudden violence
(They bear proud scars), would shoot the Elect on sight,
Unknowing that beyond the horizon's haze
Lies the world the General sought. The Elect
Beside the crystal lakes pointed with stars
Draw maps by moonlight and by firelight,
And write accounts of miracles and dangers,
Wondering how to get these to the few
Disguised as citizens or villagers,
Whose eyes must brighten and whose hearts must yearn
For these eternal heights of no return.

Sometimes the Elect, disloyal to the General,
Disgusted with the village cults whose message
Crackles on the radio when not jammed
By city static, wish him stuck in hell:
He beat his women but they cherish theirs;

His track sometimes circles back on itself
Where theirs now cuts through rigorously straight;
Their maps are no longer the same, nor is their thought.
They shun the stagnant lowlands where he fought.

Then in bad times when their supplies run low,
Night chills and loneliness making them crazed,
They yell and quarrel and threaten to throw
Each other off cliff edges, or in fear
Stumble down rock slides, paths collapsing
Under their feet. It seems that their New Age
Is founded on a love infused with rage.

At times they sense the General's eyes in theirs:
It was his restless search that brought them here
To mountain tops so passionately clear.
Sometimes on rocky paths they think they feel
His hand touching a shoulder, and they wheel
To face in ecstasy the midday sky
Where spinning waves, the vortices of time,
Whirl into points of light.
                        Do these create
Or are they sucked in by the world and breath?
This sky the General saw when facing death.

MIND, MIND

Man is nothyng but his mynd
            Bedingfield's *Cardanus's Comfort*, 1576

Nothing but mind: no, man is more than mind.
And mind creates more than more mind; this flesh,
This mesh of matter matters more than mind.
Through blind convulsions birth and love endure
And lure man on to more and more than mind.
So woman, more than man and more than mind,
Will bind him more than mind to her as more
Is born from this embrace of atoms, more
From the interstices through which mind weaves
Its dance no less than this dance of ourselves
Incarnate, O incarnate, through the mind.
Mind, mind the trembling selves we leave behind:
Nothing but mind, no thing is left to mind.

THIS MOMENT

This moment of all possibles is im-
(Don't hold your breath and die of loss
Of what was never) possible for us.
The walls unsmashable of this
Nothing here between us, only time's
Flux tubes writhe and couple – oh
Turn to me now, before I am gone:
I stifle, propped by drying bone.

PASTORAL

The Dresden shepherd to his shepherdess,
His crook upright beside her flowered hem:
'Your eyes reflect the sky . . . Ah, tenderness
Is due this heart of mine which only beats
For you, my dear . . . How delicate your cheeks,
Your mouth is like a rose . . . ' The budding horns
Nub hard beneath his curled wig as he speaks.

He thinks: I'd tear the curlicues and flowers,
I'd blunder through the lacy frills, the pleats
Of your unnecessary satin dress,
I'd tup you in the grass, cover your bleats
With bellows of exemplary fierceness,
I'd concavate my heaving, woolly paunch
Around your jutting, creamy, soft-whorled haunch . . .

He only thinks. He is a gentleman
Playing at shepherd (or a shepherd playing
At gentleman) and she a lady playing
At shepherdess (or shepherdess at lady)
– More than lusty ram and quivering ewe.
Or could it be that both are something less?
– Gentleman, lady; shepherd, shepherdess,
Playing at being more than merely sheep
Counting themselves to death to fall asleep.

DÁN

Gaelic *dán* – what is given: gift, fate, poem

A poem is a gift
From me to you,
From you to me:
This circle makes it true.

It is a ring of love
Around us both,
Of golden light
In which we pledge our troth.

It holds our bad and good,
Our dark and bright,
Our life and death,
Our insight and outsight.

Nothing but all it takes,
All you, all me:
Possession makes
Us and the poem free.

HONESTY

The parchment panes of honesty
Reflect the candlelight.
I want to make a vow
To be as straight in future
As I am, naked, now.

Pathways taken in the past
Are lost in tangled brush.
Truth's machete clears them out,
But honesty when cut
And dried relieves no doubt.

Not spectral in translucent pods
My own seed stirs within.
The candle flares to your warm flesh.
Not like this lunar relic,
Your honesty is fresh.

SOLOMON

We lie upon a hill of bones,
A thin soil over ribs and knees
And skulls from whose gone mouths the moans
Are lost in centuries.

Your cat-loose skin, your silky hips
And thighs, your breasts as in the Song
Of Solomon, your open lips
On mine will not stay long.

Your breath's a mist that fades on glass,
Your lips will fall, your breasts to dust,
Your bones to stones, your hair to grass,
Your blood to earth like rust.

ENTRANCED

How imagine the words in there?

Lynch mob jostling, each one alone
In chorus, to string the poet up
On a jacaranda flowering
With purple tongues . . .

A catacomb of dead
Who come alive at the gust of doom
Down the vaults, shivering bone,
Hobbling to the entrance . . .

They are not chosen, any more
Than the stranger who stands behind
(Rapping, rapping at) the door
Then bursts into the brain . . .

Words without name, encoded,
Electric, try to find
Each other in the mucoid tracks
And films of mind . . .

Ghostly words counted sheep
Stream to the edge of a headland
And gather in a flock till sleep
Lets them drown in woolly foam . . .

A would-be Muse calls for the knife
(Her feet in the air, lips a gash),

For a Milky Way (the Word)
In the firmament of her womb . . .

Girl and boy, in a café, knee to knee
(Muzak, the crowd's clanging), hear
Their own voice, entranced:-unspoken
Words come together in the air.

3
THE DOUBLE-GOER

THE DOUBLE-GOER

Irrational π chose an island;
Rational II (his double-goer) town,
In which to square and multiply himself,
Mirrored with whore-bums, tits, and lipsticked mouths,
And after (*'une fois philosophe . . .*) debate,
Horrored by AIDS, clap, herpes, pimp's knife-prick,
Went home (. . . *deux fois pervers'*) to masturbate.

While that absurd, irrational π,
Naked in pouring from-the-ocean rain,
Ate berries: salal-, salmon-, huckle-, black-,
Until his lips were purple with the stain,
Then scrabbling, knuckles skinned, in underbrush
Found tinder, kindling, struck a fire and blew
It high before his grinning face: uprush

Of sparks swirled to fir-tops: *She* appeared,
Her eyes like embers, hair burnished by fire,
Nipples like charcoal on Her smoky skin,
Queen of the night with π to dance and spin
As from Her lightless radiance he, the surd,
Formed circles: from the island out and round
Spread pulses of concentric heat and sound.

π's and his Love's vibrations hummed and blazed
Even through II, the square, only aware
When he awoke under a tree, numb, dazed,
Bemuddied, ashed, beside a smear of tar

Where ravens picked at small splinters of bone
A merciful soft rain was washing white,
Falling through slanted bars of morning light.

VORTICES

It was a sad journey between the islands.
In the water beside the ferry, the vortices –
Whirls of desire, worlds of desire –
Spread like galaxies across a midnight sky.
I might as well have had a telescope
So distant I was: if I turned back
And looked along the ferry deck
I saw you small and far away.
Each tiny port, entered and left in excitement,
Faded so soon under the midday sky,
My gaze returned to the vortices –
Whirls of desire, worlds of desire.

ISLANDS

Two islands but one country
We lie surrounded by a peaceful sea,
The purple sea of night.

Alpine ridges in the sheets
Are separated by dark straits.

Pacific is the pressing air
Between our bodies lying bare.

When I rise the moon is on its back
Like a silver cup in velvet black.

I cross the reddening water of dawn,
A dead volcano blocks the flaring sun.

I move into a mist of white,
Your island lost to sight.

When sun sets in our country
I return across the peaceful sea,
The purple sea of night.

DEVOURER

I brought life West with me.
My blood seeped, a river,
Corpuscles rotted with the spawn
Of salmon, dried on stone
Of dead volcano mountains
Where Pacific dawn
Glimmered the last stains:
Death in the terrains
Of promise. She, devourer,
Licks what salt remains.

AMBITION

This hopeless swimming toward the source, bashed
By waves that flush me toward a rocky shore,
Plunging my head through green walls, lashed
By strips of foam, I have no more time for:
Time is on its side, sea through which I swim.
I fight for me. I know the source is cold,
The calm relentless moon that tugs the rim
Of ocean to a standing wave. More bold
To turn my back, bruised, wade in to the strand
Of some quiet cove, and make a life away
From hissing wave-tops on the unmoving land
Where gorse clings to cliffs unsplashed by spray,
And grasshoppers in tiny glades defy
The downward crush of gravity and sky.

POOR BALL

The bronze horns found in the bog, ornamented with tiny spikes, were for religious ceremonies. Some had a hole for a now-rotted mouthpiece, not at the end but in their sides, and were almost impossible to blow. Dr. Robert Ball of Dublin did succeed in producing the one note these instruments were capable of, a deep bass sound very like the bellowing of a bull, but attempting to repeat it he burst a blood vessel and died shortly afterwards.

Aubrey Burl, *Rites of the Gods*

Poor Ball. It was a valiant death.
Blasted his brains out with his breath.
Not content with one bull bellow,
Had to try again, rash fellow.

Poor girl whose child my friend delivered:
Pushed so hard, blood vessels livered
On her face. She lived to rue it.
She didn't need to do it.

Ball, bursting for the Irish nation;
Mother of desperation
Bursting for birth: I love you both,
Bursting myself to find the truth.

We try so hard. Ball, she and I:
Perfectionists until we die.

JACK AND JENNY

The animal in us is mule to time,
Carries day's burdens on its groaning back,
Collapses every sunset, muscles slack,
Till death goads it to climb the final track . . .
Is would-be Jack, mounts Jenny, swollen member
Between her stretch-skinned haunches, hooves a-clamber,
With muted brays . . .
                            We call each other's names
And sparks from our ashes slowly rise
Through smoky spirals into lilac skies –
Exhaled not from the animal in us
But spirit: anima and animus.

GRAMMAR OF LOVE

That love may be indicative
With nothing to subjoin,
Tell the truth –
Not plead, cajole, enjoin;

And do not with imperatives
Command, forbid, or force
Dominion
Of marriage or divorce;

Now would it be conditional,
Nor bribe with 'if', require,
Or blackmail,
If true to its desire;

And lest an alien mood
Betray the naked here,
Love as is –
Not as it were:

Neither one relative,
Neither subjoined,
We clauses
Who apposite, conjoined . . .

AN IMMIGRANT

Missing an old home in a new:
Hedgerows, church spire, stone walls, primroses . . .

Dust storms come rushing through dry grass
Around the sod hut, half-built house
And hopeful shade-trees shoulder high.

Putting down roots! The wiry clumps
Of tumbleweed bowl on the ground.

The old-timer, gun on the wall,
Near death at last grows gentle
Thinking of his native land.

His hard sons own (it gave them birth)
Where they'll put him, the tussocked earth.

MANTIS

To locate the 'ear' responsible, the scientists used a process of elimination. They removed a mantis's legs and coated various parts of its body with a heavy layer of petroleum jelly or melted wax.

Science News, 15 February 1986

The praying mantis preyed upon by men:
They stick electrodes in his abdomen,
And by a process of elimination
Submit all six legs to an amputation,
Seal with petroleum each orifice,
And bombard him with ultrasound – all this
To find his single Cyclopean ear,
A breast-groove catching all he needs to hear.
It is the well-known, pitiable fate
Of mantis to be eaten by his mate.
But now there's one more thing for him to pray
For: that death comes the usual way.

CASCADES

There bricks crumble,
Woven in by grass
With chips of Roman tile
And whorled window glass.

London stone corrodes to dust,
Big Ben will fall,
And Thames will silt
The runnelled Mall.

Mansions, row houses –
Nothing will stay behind
But their debris
In a city of the mind.

Here is wilderness:
The snow-swept ridge,
The endless Alpine folds,
The distant coast a smudge.

In the volcano's ash
The wiry, hard
Roots and blades push
Through grit, prism and shard.

No cities to reduce
Where none has ever been,
Safety is in numbness,
Absorption by the scene:

Emotion as the summit's plume,
Passion as the cascades' spume.

HEDGE AND WALL

Things that grow in hedges: virgin's-bower,
Honeysuckle, guelder-roses,
Take the passer's breath.

Things that grow in walls: campanula,
Valerian, winter-in-summer,
Take the passer's eye.

What takes breath takes eye, and eye, takes breath
As you take me, my hedge, my wall:
So all takes all.

AVEBURY

Among the timeless stones what takes the eye
Is a girl on a bicycle –
Pink blouse, and black skirt riding up her thigh –
Pedalling fast
As if in danger in this place,
Through time a-race.

The church clock strikes above the chanting choir
At practice, and the doves inside their cote
Cru-crooo-cru, cru-crooo-cru, cru-crooo-cru,
Then lower – Ooo, Ooo, Ooo – throat to throat.

Impossible to tell which stones, which sheep
Against the downs from far – all seem to sleep,
Until the little ones jostle the big
To suckle and their plangent baas are heard
Quavering through the stilled air of dusk,
Circles dissolve, stones seem to push and shove –
Except the giant ones nothing will move.

Like weeping, laughing dodderers and crones
Humped or crouching in the grass, the stones
Scarred by cutting flints, eroded, lined,
Holding hands to knobbly chins, must know
More than the visitors who come and go.

As the sun sinks I mount the avenue,
Each stone a foresight for a nimbus flash.

My heart is heavy as the sun's red ball,
For at the top is (nothing?): darkness, pall.

Some stones are coupled: male to female face,
Tall-short, slim-broad – great Mammas and Papas,
Their children straggle after them in lines
Doing what they have been set to do,
Pointing out the way the centuries through.
The living (no more living?) couples pass
Between them, interweaving on the grass,
Hand in hand to watch the red sun set.
These lovers have not faced each other yet.

In the pub within the ancient ring
Yobs hit the jackpot on the fruit machine,
Neon lights flash, the jukebox flickering
As the pale barmaid hears a goddess sing:
'Taam aafter taam . . .'
Outside, the plaintive bleating of a lamb:
The dugs are dry.
The dead sun's blood is streaming in the sky
Around the spearpoints of the church's tower.
The darkened stones retain their endless power.

4
LETTER FROM NEW IRELAND

BAIE DES CHALEURS

1

Boats are locked in the harbour, ribs cracked by the ice.
How can I breathe, how can I not breathe in your arms?

The mouths of lobster traps are smothered in snow.
How can I breathe, how can I not breathe in your arms?

As a child you skated on this ocean marbled white.
How can I breathe, how can I not breathe in your arms?

Your look is cold as these gusts bringing tears to my eyes.
How can I breathe, how can I not breathe in your arms?

But I know what moves under this snow-tongued waste of
   ice:
Shoals, eddies, tendrils of anemones. You emerge
From dazzling waves in summer with diamonds and pearls
On your shoulders, hair as darkly curled as seaweed,
Eyes bright as rare black stones among the pebbles.

How can I not breathe in your arms?

2

You come on skis out of the setting sun
Toward me in a gold halo.
Your shadow lunges forward across the snow.
Your eyes are dark as your shadow.

3

Let me off this frozen sea onto the frozen land,
Across the salty slush and drifts which hide the frozen sand
To where the heads are falling off the snowmen in the thaw
And spruces stretch themselves to snap their manacles of ice
As I stretch out to you in clouds of breath my melting hand.

4

The bay thaws: cloud grey, drizzle grey, water grey,
Floes white, mist above a snowy point white,
Seagulls on the floes white and grey –
A film of white and grey.

I thaw with the sea in your arms.

In an old colour film you are belle of the ball,
Of graduation, Christmas *réveillon* –
Erect, high-cheekboned, an Indian princess,
Slow but with moments of quickness.

I move with the sea in your arms.

Your sudden smile, a flash of sun,
Lights up this world: there is no cloud,
You are as dazzling as the summer sea
And sparkling as the tumbling waves.

I pound with the sea in your arms.

LETTER FROM NEW IRELAND

October: still the yellow butterflies
Dawdle around the yellow dandelions.
Asters, like nebulas of Venuses,
Drift in the field. Propeller search planes drone –
Like Lancasters returning to Belfast
After the war. The airmen here wear green
And hate it. As in that artsy poem by Frost,
This soft morning was mild etc. Am I obscene?
I've found my femme fatale. My thinning hair
Reveals the scar I got that otherwise
(I smashed the windscreen when an A30
Hit black ice on the Malone Road, then a tree).
I'm not unhappy. Under this green sod
Perhaps a home awaits. If there's a God
He's in me (so I feel, without disproof
Until I take the thunderbolt of truth).
'Dog is God backwards,' my daughters say,
'Dad can bark like a dog.' I'll have my day,
Then under dandelion-dappled sky
Of aster blue, a sleeping dog I'll lie.
My youngest climbed the shed roof in the garden
To pick some pears and told us 'they taste golden'.
Son of a bitch, I could be, but I think I'm
The last in the New World to bark in rhyme.
Here they pronounce Dad, 'Dead'. A woman said,
'Whenever he was dronk he'd lay in the bid
And roar. Oi always loved moi dead.' I like

It here. Maybe in time we'll go back West.
All the best –

PS The postal workers are on strike.

YOU AND ISLAND

You land, wind-bitten, blood-rusted
Earth ice-crumbled, shores wave-eaten,
Time against you – you'll outlast men
(Thus me) but will be outlasted
By continents whose snow-peaks shine
In sun. Once under sea, you rose,
Will sink again, and (who knows?)
Rise pink in an age far from mine,
Small hills enough for children's suck,
Curved beaches open to the salt-chuck –
Sky, sea and little land (you and
Island), breakers dying on your sand.

MAN

On the point, a man, the foresight of a gun,
Bisects the orange of the setting sun.
His shadow strikes a black line on the sand,
Cut at the neck by the next rusty headland.
Wild rose and clover scents in his nose
Mingle with other smells he'd like to lose.
Naked, though not so clean, as a baby
He'll plunge into the shimmering sea
Perhaps to be reborn as more than I
To face the lemon moon, its cold sky.

WAVES

I swim through waves of pearly-everlasting,
Hollows of grass – timothy, vetch, clover,
Cobwebs' lacy nets, plashes of goldenrod –
Then gasping climb surf mountains whose snow-crests
Topple on my head and plunge me into dark –
Howls in my ears like panic in the woods,
A naked flight through fireweed – then out to sky
And loss, loss, loss. Better to hold it in –
Pain, confusion – without her, better dead
Than waves of flowers breaking through old skin.

COUSINS SHORE

Bury me by Cousins Shore
In sand my head to cover
When I will be no more
And loose my soul to hover
(If I have one) and face
As dead kings used to do
(I a dead thing) the North,
The sapphire Gulf where terns
Plummet and plash, whose spray
Will sweep my ghostly vapour
Across the marram grass,
Dunes, poison ivy, roses,
Ditches hemmed with Queen Anne's lace,
To settle, baneful dew,
On fields of carnal clover –
Unless my soul, alone,
Undrownable in eyes
For which my flesh once died,
Will live as death, a sense
(No, Donne, death never dies)
Of something frightening
To couples under blankets
For skin-warmth snuggling,
The sand between their toes,
Pink sand of Cousins Shore
That oh how pleasantly
Has cleaned my flesh from bone
The couples may discover:

At dusk it gleams sepulchral
But will in time like shell
Be sand, long lost my voice,
The fleeping of a plover
Swerving quick to skim
The waves around my head,
Bobbing as alone I swim
Here in the sea, rejoice
That I am not yet dead.

MICMAC WOMAN

Mouth like a bow, eyes angular like arrows,
Face like a heart, teeth like the white cemetery
Slabs rain-spit above the wind-torn narrows,
Breasts like the war memorial cairn's round
Stones, high laugh like a gull's (in cloud-mist) cry,
Brown hair dark-streaked like December ground
Muddy between the frosts. The memory
Of other islands in another sea
Draws me away from her. Mouth like a bow
And back tensed like a bow, her aim's not me.
Soon the sheets of rain will turn to snow.

DIELAND

Take this island
All for yourself –
Make it your dieland:
Winter ice-locked,
Swirled wastes of snow
Dimpled and pocked,
Crossed by the barbed-wire
Fences of desire.

TERRA FIRMA

Seen from an island, islands in the air
Upside down, blue coastlines above white
Plateaus in the wavy atmosphere,
Mirror blue of water, white of floe.
Where we are is no more terra firma.
Seen from those floating islands in the air,
Two moving upright specks would blur to one
Dancing dot in the mirage, then disappear
On upside-down snow plateaus hit by sun.

THANK-YOU NOTE

My birthday present. You. I unwrap you,
Untie the ribbons, open up the gift:
All you. For me. I speak to you in tongues,
A church spire teeters in iridian skies
The sun leaps through, snow flowers on the hedges,
The wrapping torn like petals on the bed,
And in your hair I bury my bald head.

DEBT

I have put down
My last halfpenny,
My last half-crown,
But these are currency
Acceptable to none,
Must be put away –
Halfpennies as copper,
Half-crowns as silver –
Against an evil day
When I'll be gone.
How can I pay
In the country
Of you? What specie
Is legal tender?
At least let me know
How much I owe.

SUNSTRUCK

to my father, Desmond Haldane, who was with
the 51st Highland Division at Alamein and after

Dead crabs (burned-out tanks in desert wars),
Spongy mats of dried salt-frosted eelgrass,
Razor-clam shells, quahogs, mussels – no spoors
Of animals, but arrow tracks of birds,
A plastic bucket, a 7-Up bottle,
Streaks of guano, two dead skate gull-gutted,
Sandpipers scuttling hunchbacked at the brink,
Out in the bay at least two hundred
Canada geese honking like Gabriel hounds,
A new V landing, tails down (bombers),
Posts along the dunes (chevaux-de-frise)
To stop them drifting (camouflaged bunkers),
The (bayonets) marram grass . . . I saw all these,
But when I doubled back around the spit –
To waves and waves of air above the waves –
My shadow leapt out sharp in front of me:
I had thought I was alone, but sunstruck
He had dogged me all along the inner shore,
And now he streaked along the strand, briskly
Dipping his head in the breakers' foam
(At a rifle pace, one hundred and twenty
A minute, a demobbed soldier) heading –
To fresh-flowered sheets, or a rumpled bed?
To welcome or disdain from her?– for home.

ICY ROAD

Driving the icy road
Of desire,
Music on the radio,
Better have good tires,

Don't lose your feel
Bucking through
Tongues of snow,
Gentle the wheel,

Keep your eyes
On what's ahead,
Don't gun uphill,
Don't brake downhill

Or you'll spin off
Into a ditch,
Turn upside down,
End in a drift,

Or crash a wall
Or worst of all
Meet your double
Coming at you

Round a curve
Out of control . . .

Keep your nerve,
Go with the road . . .

As you keep moving
It moves too
Though where it goes
Nobody knows.

THE MURMUR

The murmur has become a shout
Let me out, out, out!
The beating has become a din
Of hellish klaxons under skin,
The heart in its little room
Bursting in a bloody tomb
Of macerated bits of pain
– Not again, again, again.
I did this to you, my chest
Once one to one on your breast
Removed a world away – gone,
You left there, heart cracking bone.
The murmur has become a shout
'Let me out, out, out
To you my love who hurt me so
Again you've let me go.'
I let you go and like a stone
I dropped over the horizon
Away from sunset-bloodied West
From you I said I loved best.
My murmur has become a shout
Let me out, out, out.
My flown-back bird has found its nest,
I hear your heart through your breast,
My murmur has become a moan
Let me home, home, home.

ACCENTS

Seán and Gisèle (Ghislaine)

My accent acute
Your accent grave –
How should we behave?

If you come first
The accent on your *e*
Points away
From the accent on my *a*,
We lean apart -- a V.

If I come first
The accent on my *a*
Points to you,
The accent on your *e*
Points to me
As you follow,
A circumflex.

As we reach to join,
Acute and grave
Curved lovingly,
We become concave
Or convex.

Or as we superpose,
E on *a*, *a* on *e*,

Our accents make an X
Of you and me.

So accents form no bar –
Whether or not we suit
Entirely, or behave
Well – to what we are:
Grave beyond the acute,
Acute beyond the grave.

QUINCE

1

Who is the brown man raking leaves,
The russet camouflage-man who wades
As if harvesting kelp in rusty billows?
Who is the quince woman in yellow
Who rescues the aromatic fruit
From trampling under his boot,
For jelly or for marmalade?
Is he good for her or bad?
He unnerves her by day, she dare
Not turn her back or he'll jump her
As he does at night, treading, lost
In scent of crushed quince, her tree bare,
Wet with dew by dawn become a frost.
Who is the quince woman who grieves?
Who is the brown man raking leaves?

2

Who could have guessed the thorny quince
Whose golden fruit, though good for jam,
Puckered our lips and made us wince
Would, shrivelled on the bough, become
So hard, so sure, each wrinkled pome
(The one you gave me as a talisman,
An aromatic nut or stone)
Seeming eternal, and that next year
After the winter stripped it bare

The tree would throw its limbs open
With blossom so like your lips, crimson
And mauve with the rush of new blood,
The stamen pushing through its tiny hood?